AMAZING SCIENCE

# Shapes in the Sky
## A Book About Clouds

by Josepha Sherman    illustrated by Omarr Wesley

Thanks to our advisers for their expertise, research, knowledge, and advice:

Mark W. Seeley, Ph.D., Professor of Meteorology and Climatology
Department of Soil, Water, and Climate
University of Minnesota, St. Paul

Mike Graf, M.A., Instructor of Child Development
Chico (California) State University

Susan Kesselring, M.A., Literacy Educator
Rosemount-Apple Valley-Eagan (Minnesota) School District

PiCTURE WiNDOW BOOKS
Minneapolis, Minnesota

Managing Editor: Bob Temple
Creative Director: Terri Foley
Editors: Sara E. Hoffmann, Michael Dahl
Editorial Adviser: Andrea Cascardi
Copy Editor: Laurie Kahn
Designer: Nathan Gassman
Page production: Picture Window Books
The illustrations in this book were rendered digitally.

Picture Window Books
5115 Excelsior Boulevard
Suite 232
Minneapolis, MN 55416
1-877-845-8392
www.picturewindowbooks.com

Printed in the United States of America.

**Library of Congress Cataloging-in-Publication Data**
Sherman, Josepha.
Shapes in the sky : a book about clouds / by Josepha Sherman ;
illustrated by Omarr Wesley. v. cm. — (Amazing science)
Includes bibliographical references and index.
Contents: What makes a cloud?—Cumulus clouds—
Cumulonimbus clouds—Stratus clouds—Cirrus clouds—
Cool days, warm nights—Clouds and Earth.
ISBN 1-4048-0097-2 (hardcover)
ISBN 1-4048-0341-6 (paperback)
1. Clouds—Juvenile literature. [1. Clouds.] I. Wesley, Omarr,
ill. II. Title.
QC921.35 .S48 2003
551.57′6—dc21
                                    2003004713

# Table of Contents

Clouds curl across the sky like dragons. They sail above the trees like scoops of vanilla ice cream.

Clouds float and fly in all shapes and sizes.

## What Makes a Cloud?

Clouds are made of trillions
of tiny water droplets and ice crystals.
These droplets and crystals hang in the air.
They are so light that even the smallest breeze
can keep them from falling to the earth.

Clouds can look as solid as mountains,
but they are as light as smoke.

Clouds drift and shift. They stretch across the sky.

Winds push the clouds and change their shapes.

## Cumulus Clouds

Scientists have names for different types of clouds.

Cumulus clouds are full and puffy.

They are piled up like heaps of whipped cream.

They often appear on summer days.

## Cumulonimbus Clouds

Cumulonimbus clouds can make hail or stir up tornadoes. Lightning flashes deep inside them. Thunder rumbles through their thick billows.

These clouds also are called thunderheads.

Cumulonimbus clouds can be
as tall as 60,000 feet (18,288 meters).
That's twice as tall as the world's highest mountain.

14

## Stratus Clouds

Stratus clouds hang low in the sky.

They hide the tops of hills and tall buildings.

Stratus clouds often appear in the winter.

They can bring raindrops or flakes of snow.

## Cirrus Clouds

When a cloud rises very high, it reaches cooler air. If the air is cool enough, the water droplets inside the cloud freeze into tiny ice crystals. Trillions of these crystals hang together and form cirrus clouds.

Cirrus clouds float high in the air, sometimes above the other clouds. They can look as wispy as feathers. They can curl like lizard tails.

## Cloudy Days, Cloudy Nights

Cloudy days are often cooler than clear days.

The clouds keep sunlight from warming the earth.

Cloudy nights are warmer than clear nights.
As the sun sets, the land and oceans cool off.
The clouds keep heat near the
ground like a giant lid.

## All the Clouds in the Sky

Some clouds swirl like fog against treetops.

Some float above mountains.

Some bring thunder and rain.

Some sail high in the sky, riding the fastest winds.

Can you see all the different types of clouds?

# You Can Make a Cloud

**What you need:**

- an ice-cube tray
- water
- a metal dish
- a jar
- a flashlight

**What you do:**

1. Make sure you have an adult help you.

2. Fill the ice-cube tray with water and place in the freezer overnight.

3. Take several ice cubes out of the tray and place them in the metal dish.

4. Let the ice cubes stand in the dish until the dish is really cold.

5. Pour 1 inch (2½ centimeters) of warm water in the jar.

6. Take the jar of water and the dish of ice cubes into a darkened room.

7. Using a flashlight to shine light on the dish and the jar, place the dish over the top of the jar.

8. Watch as a cloud forms near the top of the jar as the warm water evaporates, rises, and then condenses.

# Fast Facts

- Fog is a cloud that is near the ground. So even if you've never flown through the clouds in an airplane, you probably know what a cloud looks like up close.

- If you spot a cloud that is tall, billowy, and dark at the bottom, be careful! Clouds like these can mean a storm is coming. Storms can bring lightning, strong winds, and even hail. During a storm, you should go indoors and stay away from windows.

- More than 200 years ago, an Englishman named Luke Howard named the different types of clouds. He loved clouds so much that people called him the Godfather of Clouds.

- Clouds always move in the sky. On a breezy day, the wind makes the clouds move faster. By watching which way a cloud moves, you can tell which way the wind is blowing.

# Glossary

**breeze**—a gentle wind

**cirrus cloud**—a cloud made of trillions of tiny ice crystals

**cumulonimbus cloud**—a huge cloud that can bring hail and tornadoes

**cumulus cloud**—a puffy white cloud that appears on summer days

**ice crystal**—a tiny frozen water droplet

**stratus cloud**—a cloud that hangs low in the sky and often brings drizzle or snowflakes

**water droplet**—a small drop of water

# To Learn More

## At the Library

Burke, Jennifer S. *Cloudy Days.* New York: Children's Press, 2000.

De Paola, Tomie. *The Cloud Book: Words and Pictures.* New York: Holiday House, 1975.

Saunders-Smith, Gail. *Clouds.* Mankato, Minn.: Pebble Books, 1998.

## On the Web

FactHound offers a safe, fun way to find Web sites related to this book. All of the sites on FactHound have been researched by our staff.

1. Visit *www.facthound.com*
2. Type in this special code: 1404800972
3. Click on the FETCH IT button.

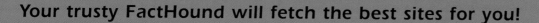

Your trusty FactHound will fetch the best sites for you!

## Index